10 Ways to Meditate

D1141982

My eye conversed
while my tongue gazed.
My ear spoke
and my hand listened.
And while my ear was an eye
to behold everything visible,
my eye was an ear listening to song.
                    —Ibn-ul-Farid

"why the ink paintings?"

brushed-on
black-ink flow
let flow
shows something

"what?"

do this:
draw a line
wholly
on paper
or wall
or air

aren't we drawing
such lines whenever
we move?

10 WAYS
TO MEDITATE

words and pictures by PAUL REPS

BONUS EDITION

WEATHERHILL : New York & Tokyo

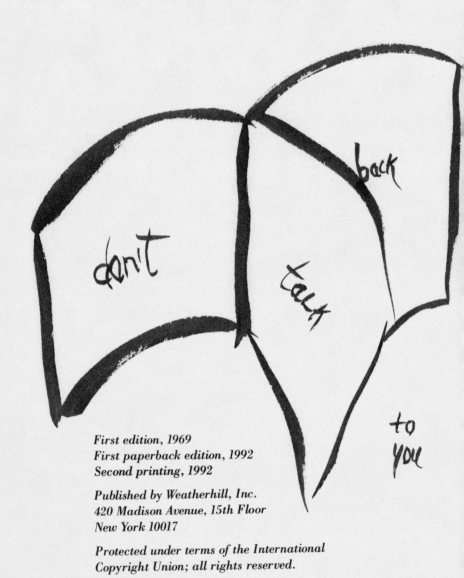

First edition, 1969
First paperback edition, 1992
Second printing, 1992

Published by Weatherhill, Inc.
420 Madison Avenue, 15th Floor
New York 10017

Protected under terms of the International
Copyright Union; all rights reserved.

Printed in Mexico

LCC Card No. 70-83639
ISBN 0-8348-0256-2

CONTENTS

meditate:
to think deeply   to reflect
turns into searching INquiry
into who I am

← bonus insert

the ways tendered here
are beginning ones
easy to do they may
not be done uneasily
the best way for you
is yours

LIST OF INK PAINTINGS

to begin:

to open inner doors
men of many races and times
have used meditation   magic   prayer
as we now use science to open
doors outwardly

how shall you open your doors?
this book tries to give ways briefly
as tonal notes for your playing

should one meditate?
the answer is NO
if it isolates us from mankind

the answer is YES
1) if done innocently
2) if it melts instead of solidifies my-ness
3) if played experimentally
4) if born momently anew

don't stop here

From
everywhere
Living
on earth

COMPLETELY RELEASE ME

through the ages man has invoked
his fount of being and left images
of himself doing so

what are those buddhas doing there?
what are those shivas and sages
and egyptians doing in the great
museums of the world?
why were they carried so far from home?
to show us something?

what do they sit and stand for
honey-eyed   inward smiling   with soft
straight back   in balance   slightly
forward   flexive yet firm?
we may too?

*in japan there is a practice of sitting on one's feet as in kneeling with the back
straight and still   it is found most beneficial but is not named meditation or even
still sitting so one is feel-free to do it freely without any mind-bind   when something is named and formalized the adventure of doing it may be (s)mothered*

TO STILL
TO BLISS THIS
COMPLETELY RELEASE ME

lie down   shoes off
s t r e t c h
release face
neck   shoulders
middle   back
me   the one who says me
then

SIT
facing a wall
forward on a low seat
both feet on ground
or crosslegged on a cushion
easy   erect   seeing released
as completely un-me'd
as when lying down
STILL

*"bliss?"   nerve juice   blood juice   lymph juice   enzyme juice
sex juice   sweat juice=life juice*

continue

mind
stills

as mind   attention
stills

IT-IS-AS-IT-IS
presently

"is that all?"

who is there
to ask for more?

experience this   let this experience you   we sit to rest   as we still we inpower
ordinary sitting uses energy   extraordinary still instills energy   generates
regenerates rejuvenates   only turning off as we move then begin again
open this immediate door opening IN

you have
a pile of books
in your arms
startled
you drop them
this instant
you're meditating

you help someone
in some small way
you're meditating

leaving dream
into deep sleep
you're meditating

you sit crosslegged
like a buddha
you're *not* meditating
why?
because your mind
is itching
that itch

minding is good too
meditating is good too

an insect hums
you become it
a bird sings
you become it
you're meditating

Chinese characters show a poem by Liu Shih-chieh, of Hong Kong,
in the poet's own calligraphy. Rough translation: "When a light breeze

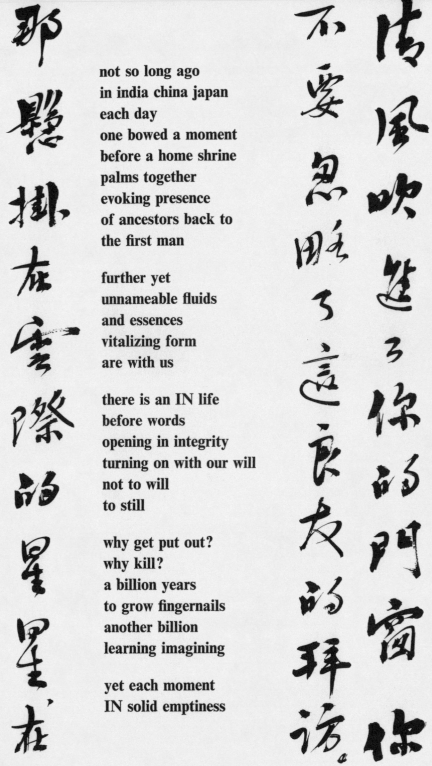

那
飄
掛
在
雲
際
的
星
星，
在

清
風
吹
進
了
你
的
門
窗
你

不
要
忽
略
了
遠
良
友
的
拜
訪。

not so long ago
in india china japan
each day
one bowed a moment
before a home shrine
palms together
evoking presence
of ancestors back to
the first man

further yet
unnameable fluids
and essences
vitalizing form
are with us

there is an IN life
before words
opening in integrity
turning on with our will
not to will
to still

why get put out?
why kill?
a billion years
to grow fingernails
another billion
learning imagining

yet each moment
IN solid emptiness

blows through the window, do not neglect its advent: stars hanging in
the clouds disclose their meditation of you in their incessant twinklings."

Stones
once were men
who sat to
become them

ENTER BREATH

experiment

if you are being breathed
10 breaths a minute
600 an hour   14400 a day
take one play day for your
breath of breath

with heart pause   breath pause   with single nerve pulse

15

eyes closed
or half closed
seeing released
l e t   breathe
as you let wind blow
rain fall

enter
one breath
WHOLLY

going with not against THE harmony

"am I already in my breath of life?"
who could be out of it?
we only think us put out

STILL
sit

l e t
breathe

are in themselves deep meditating
before we name them
before we do them
on a day without complaint

before-ing troubling melts

if the human race (you) is (are) mad (with desires) the act of still sanitizes
and puts you in breath where you belong to live long and well

at home with light and dark

until its
Fun
better left
undone

18

INLISTEN

"do we need a teacher?"
we need each one   each presence
each experience teaches us something
more we need response to our
fount of BEing

there is no substitute for inner
guidance   our dearest teacher
intuitively within   even when without
in our re-act

we use intuitive guidance to make a choice   to walk across a room
to think   to gesture   women are rich in it
this same intuitive turns inward to our source of be-ing
in fact we never are away from our source
so established nothing is the matter

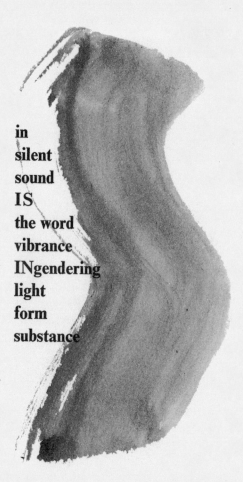

in
silent
sound
IS
the word
vibrance
INgendering
light
form
substance

ultra sound as HUU in coo of dove   purr of cat   hum of motor   in wind
bell   gong   tone of sea   do it lightly   when the child in us no longer feels
moves plays draws freely (after about 5 years of age) when spontaneity dulls and
guilt shame formalisms are imposed   then the imposer joins the living dead
what is an answer for you?   another imposition?

wheat in the field has been found
to grow better with music   sound waves
we grow with silent sound   integrity

do we listen   really listen?
to what?   to put out meanings?
nationalism   internationalism   racism
me-ism   as concepts incite us

to purify me is possible
to melt think into love is possible
we are doing it most of the time
when we are not doing it

seeds knows   root knows   sprout knows
in   silent   sound

seeing
you
my hair
stands
on end

INLIGHT

what we do formally
we freeze
what we do informally
we free

touch finger to forehead
both object-ing and subject-ing

between these
the indescribable experience

Far
down
your line
of light
your order
will be
filled

let
INlight
turn on

sit in sun
or in the light of dark
seeing released

in INlight
consciousness
be
light

"how?"   before how   pore see   wholly see   INlight is instant
it reaches through all space   we are made of lightpoints   "what is light?"
infrontofyouinbackoverunderaroundisthis LIGHT

being alone makes possible
being alone together

what we ask
into the aroma of a flower
or a stick of incense
may turn us upsidedown
so that all we have falls
out of pockets and
everything is all right

BRIGHT

how seriously a child plays insideout perfuming the atmosphere for miles around
clap hands for the gigantic cellebration of seed and flower
helpless helpful to do anything but seed and flower

to say   what it is

weeding

would be like

sewing a label   on a flower

Flowering

or tying a purse   to a bird

we pass

to say   what it is not

your door

would only be   another   tying

MOVE STILL

a seed   a small thing
potentials a huge tree

a man   a small thing
potentials in-finiting
grace

as breath flows out   tighten
as breath flows in   o p e n

in exertion we soon self-learn to move with breath
when we forget then impulse moves us out and lost
we tire and don't know what's the matter
plenty is the matter moving against ourself

cultivating the breath of life is the work of every plant
shall we be less than a plant?

when moving
do not disturb
the breath

move with it
smooth
even

continued motion without acceleration or deceleration feels like dancing
our nerve-muscle network likes such unusual kindness
consider motion in motion

A BONUS OF FOUR ONES:

One Moment That Lasts Forever

One Supreme Way to Turn On Our In-light

One Cellebration

And one scroll for you . . .

One Moment That Lasts Forever

In talking about meditation during my visit to India, a man who had been a chronic alcoholic and a dope addict . . . related that one day he had met a holy man. (There are about two million roaming the country in India.) The holy man told him that all he had to do was to still the wheels of his mind and for about half an hour, twice a day, affirm: "Brahma's love, peace, beauty, glory and light are flowing through my whole being, purifying, cleansing, healing and restoring my soul."

He followed the instructions, knowing that he would activate and resurrect the qualities and powers of God resident in his subjective depths. He continued meditating every night and morning; and at the end of a few weeks, while meditating one night, his whole mind and body, as well as the room he was in, became a blaze of light. He was actually blinded, as was Paul, by the light for awhile. He felt an inner rapture and ecstasy and a sense of oneness with God and the whole world. His feeling was indescribable.

He had experienced what the ancient mystics called "the moment that lasts forever." He was completely healed and is teaching others how to lead a new life. He invested his mind wisely—that is real meditation.

—Joseph Murphy's "Within You Is the Power," p. 75 (DeVorss, 1977)

One Supreme Way to Turn On Our In-light

"How do I do this?"
As easy as A, B, C.

–A–

WE ARE MADE OF LIGHT
visible and in-visible
with countless stars
we see turning
rhythmically as suns
and suns of suns
in this
lightness.

As we accept this,
as we receive this,
we see ourselves rightly
as made of uncountable
lightpoints
one with our whole
be-ing indescribably
near   dear.

–B–

"How do I do it?"
Do no-thing but
receive

your life-gift
to you of you.

With subdued exertion
on natural outbreathflow
your _in_breathflow
returns rhythmically
heaping from body base
to tophead with
indescribable
lightness.

As you become the
lightness
you ARE, other feel it.
Such giving—radiating—
increases your receiving

-C-

Do not make this mysterious
or difficult. Play it.
If is the truth of our
packaging cosmos in a
grassblade, as the freeing
spirit of children,
as the flight of birds,
we earn by sweating—each atom
intepenetrating each other atom.

So much is given us for
sharing.

Tell others but in your own
words. This is as simple as
turning, turning to the love-
harmony-beauty through your
breathflow you already are
in and of.

Let do.
Enter the motion silently
saturating all nature,
our nature.
Moving silently we simply
replace outgoing mind-
attention with IN
and IN this sure moving
we let all pressure off our
face, now somehow a new face
in a new world as we move
wholly.

Is this hard to understand?
It may seem so when we move
against ourselves, against our
constrictions.
Light saturates
and frees self-imposed
constrictions as we let it.

"How does this relate
to others? How do you
know it? How do you know

it is not other than as
you see-say it?"

We abide in our
infiniting.
Each grassblade tries to
be a perfect grassblade—
and succeeds. Our
possibilities are unlimited
and unlimiting.

You also may enter
through sounds.
Fingers in ears, in-hear
your natural hum,
hmmmmmmmmmmmmmmmmmmmmmmmm.

Silently feel this
hmmmmmmmmmmmmmmmmmmmmmmmmmm
with breathflow out-in out-in
some 22,000 times daily,
extending breathflow slightly,
increasing oxygen assimilation
in deep peace so you live longer
growing younger silently
self-directively,
wholeheartedly.

hmmmmmmmmmmmmmmmmmmmmmm
hmmmmmmmmmmmmmmmmmmmmmm
hmmmmmmmmmmmmmmmmmmmmmmm

Dear Reps,

    Each day I breathe
as you showed me. Already
I feel new. Billions of
tiny voices in my tissues
cellebrating light.
    Thank you.

           Much love,
           Sally

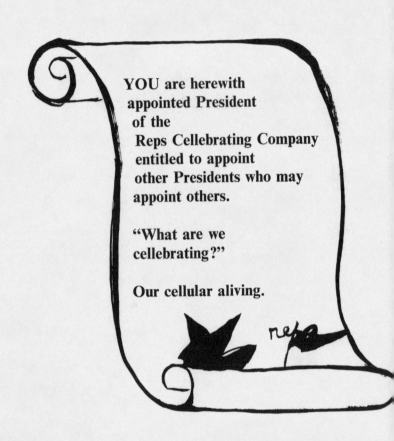

YOU are herewith
appointed President
of the
Reps Cellebrating Company
entitled to appoint
other Presidents who may
appoint others.

"What are we
cellebrating?"

Our cellular aliving.

to stand still
to move still
we will to do it
then are willing

by will we kill
another or ourself
still
we will not to will

it is so easy
we make it uneasy
to prove it

cup hands   stretch high   moving slowly at the same rate of speed let palms
pass without touching over head   forehead   face   neck   torso   legs
feet   our + − flow awaits our guidance

forcing is not the way   indulgence is not the way   YOU are the way

out of breath a thought comes to you   you ask "are we killers? we kill thousands
of bloodcells each day making way for new ones   we kill as we think   step
chew   we organize group killings   shall we meditate this?"

are we killers or transmuters?   we are children of the one mother   atomically
electro-magnetically   there is no killer or killed but an ever transmuting   every-
one is busy becoming everyone else   we ARE together   isn't it wonderful

how can two
sleeping in
the same bed
have the same
dream

WAKE

we are mostly asleep when awake

"is it possible to sleep awarely?"

we say I had a sound sleep
so we must be aware of it innately
though not divisibly
senses do not sense until we INsense
why scatter into matter?

"who suffers?   kills?   is killed?"

no one
it's a dream

"then how do we wake from this dream?"

you already ARE awake

waking from dream we have no more concern
with the dream participants
waking from daydream we have no more concern
with the daydream participants

wake

wake

WAKE

body becomes mind   mind becomes whatever is in it
and when its load gets too heavy
born again is like waking

easy as play   when awake
considerately   wholly release
consider   nerveflow
deep   bloodflow
sleep   any thought
    and
early at night   enter
enter   your
deep   BEing
sleep
awake

in usual sleep   *"is this my being?"*
we are unaware of it
until afterwards   *why ask me*
in sleep awake   *why not ask your me*
aware   *pre-conceiving*
we do not re-act   *unborn*
    eternal
    pervasive
    here

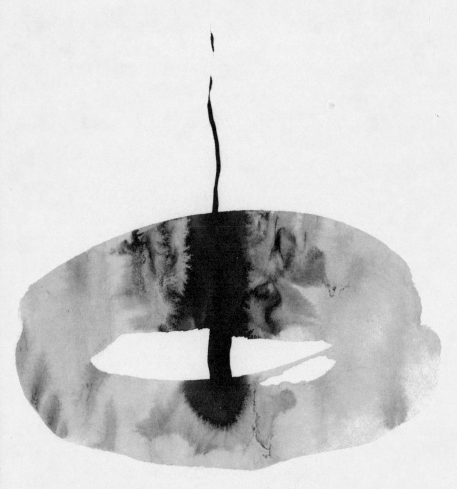

pooL
of
thud

7

SILENCING

each evening
silently
observe
any thought
any feel

so simple
delightful
very peaceful too

life is beyond closed comprehension name form
and absolutely inescapable
every product of man is spiced with error

do this

actualise
space

silently

in this
SILENCING
aware

word spoken
returns to
SILENCING

a thought
becomes
all thought

busy
intertastes
still

in your
SILENCING
presence

more   than   yours

insee stairs
as if stepping down
from above
then suddenly
as if from underneath
the posts shifting
from far to near
faster than thought
IN the shift
not above not below
not far
not near
IN

INCHANT

8

"GOOD"

a sound heard
also is self-made
a pre-sound pre-heard
initiates the inner life

we approve of us   there must be some deep reason for this   for grass growing
INsinging   INsing some silent word on breaths   "what word?"   any word is
good as you make it so   perhaps GOOD or GOOD GOOD GOOD

positively

deep in
each one feels
I AM

who is this
innate I AM?

I AM
the heart
of each one

receptively

small i
fits into BIG I
as hand in glove
as wave in sea
immediately

though bodies come and go I AM never has been known to change   does it not
follow that "I choose and am responsible for my thought and action"?
yes   I AM.

40

wave
re-turns
to sea

wave : our separative self
sea : our native thought-free state
        giving oneself as another
        as water flowing   as effacing
        of a sleepless child   as leaf
        in wind
        effacing as greatest possible refreshment

planning?
scheming?

take a
little
walk

ACCORDINGLY

"why do we live?"

to re-present ourselves
to go with it

"how?"

we are impacted
with innumerable sound vibrances
we never hear
with myriad lightpoints
we never see

wherever we are
as we are
ten thousand impresses
come through
although we may be aware
of only a few

these few are for you
let it
whatever it is
through

without re-acting to it
without imposing any value judgment on it
without weighing or saying it
simply receive

and
selfmade knots
let go

and
it has no resistance
from us
so it passes through
so life passes through
free of me

IN perfect be-ing

living
at
altitude

MIND OF LIGHT

when from some overnegative or overpositive re-act we
tighten up   then it knots in our back   anyone can feel
it as this knot is steadily pressed   (mother presses
child)   it lets go and the congested organ and breath
let go to feel better   such let go precludes hurry worry
and may be learned from any cat

what we do often contradicts our basic slow nerve
rhythm under heart rhythm   then we shorten our life
with forcing fearing   confusion   how dangerous we
are   instead of spending energy for what why not
release do in the do as they do in green city ching cheng
in szechuan province in china where so many men and
women 150 to 400 years of age live at altitude   eat
lightly   focussing spirit life with the spirit of heaven
and earth perfectly normally

we explored all out
turn IN?

as m i n d
by its very nature free
I am free of me

as me however
possessing dream
and daydream
I make myself
plenty of trouble

instead of hunting
ways out
hunt for you

find no pinned you
too aliving
to pin down
or up

laughingly

"looking inward
I find
no
thing
but
being"

come closer

experience this
experience that
now

experiencing
experiencing

a naked jump into our immaterial pool of joy   jump

in the
mind
of light
one does
not die

constant   changeless   boundless   whole

THERE IS

there is a state of formlessness in form
      toss a string or string of beads in air
      and as it rests in beauty
      read the picture there
there is the state of love
      clap hands
      which hand was the clapper?
      make the other one the clapper
      now make both   that's love
there is a state of bliss   of reality
      stand with both feet parallel
      let eyes close
      feel weight more on one foot then the other
      as weight comes to exact center you disappear
      this IS bliss
there is a state of perfect peace
      sit most comfortably erect
      let eyes close

quiet alert

feeling the weight more on one sit bone
then the other
equally on both bones
you're in peace
there is a state of cosmos consciousness
let move in evenly timed rhythm
without stopping or breaking
or accelerating
or decelerating
as the sunrise
there is one light equally for everyone
one love
there is one sound
one silent sound
opening the flowers and weeds
filling all needs
there is a state of BEing
just BE and you're IN it

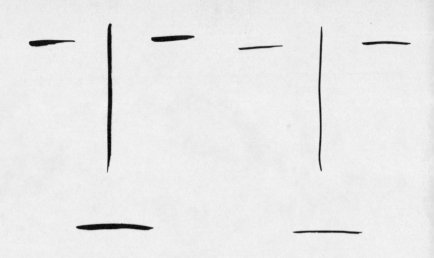

some questions, some answers "but *how* do I meditate? exactly what do I do?" you don't   you *let* do it   it is built in   you are doing it already innately   in sleep   in moving   in sitting still   all nature is meditating in adoration of its BEing   only we humans spoil it by tightening up on ourselves and disturbing our great peace   "is it *that* easy?"   not when you make it hard   so let us review our ways:

1. completely release me   lie down and let go   then sit still as much at ease as when lying flat   just like a cat   "but what do I do with my thoughts?"   do nothing   as you still let thoughts still   they will   in still you begin to rejuvenate

2. "how can I be still when I am breathing?"   never breathe just let breath breathe in its own rhythm   let   let   l e t

3. "but I hear sounds"   let them through   as an experiment put fingers in ears to inlisten to biorhythmic tone   inlisten as a root to insound   so near   so far away   you do not hear but feel it

4. "do I do this in the dark?"   dark or light   let your insight turn on   at first imagine you are made of innumerable lightpoints as you are turn on your bright

5. "but I must move"   naturally   when you are moved   only don't move against yourself   let move smooth gently even IN moving is meditating too

6. "how can I wake when I am already awake?" let wake more
love it   wake to inmost you as well as to outer things   waking
is BEing

7. "is silencing the same as still?"   in still our whole life is given
us   sometimes in silencing it becomes powerfully invibrant
presence

8. "is this good?"   inchant "good" and discover for you   no
one can do it for you   we are both wave and sea   don't miss
your sea effacingly

9. "but I have many responsibilities"   we all have   but don't
lose response-ability   going with it

10. "have we a mind of light?"   we do not have mind   we *are*
mind   you may name light or insound vibrance or whatever you
choose   experiencing is more than naming   more than thinking
more even than BEing   or effacing   this more let through you

"is there a school where I can learn this?"   yes   yes   wherever
you are   whatever you are doing   teacher and learner are in
you   10?   10,000 ways to learn and teach and INreach   thank
you for your life

direct
experience